"A love story played with fierce sincerity and unexpected honesty."

—*Wall Street Journal*

"The musical has a masterful, even revelatory, book by the Irish playwright Enda Walsh . . . it is no traditional screen-to-stage adaptation. Rather, it's a textbook example of how to do it right. Everything you see, hear and feel is inherently theatrical . . . you start to feel things the movie simply could not make you feel. The characters deepen, and their dilemmas seem to pulse directly to you."

—*Chicago Tribune*

"Beautiful."

—*New York* magazine

"The sweetest and most romantic show on Broadway . . . Spanning a week in Dublin, the story is deceptively simple and speaks volumes about the power of music and connection."

—*Daily News*

"Original and emotionally exhilarating, *Once* is the sort of revivifying breeze nowhere more necessary than on Broadway."

—*Washington Post*

"*Once* is unusually fun and heartfelt musical theater."

—*New Yorker*

"Heart-stopping and enthralling. It's a genuine thrill to hear an entire Broadway house hushed and focused on the action onstage. And it makes the roar of applause at the end all the more ecstatic."

—Huffington Post

"A rhapsodic, unique musical that retains all the heart of the original Irish film."

—*Variety*

"*Once* in a blue moon, perhaps *Once* in a decade or so, a new Broadway musical breaks the rules, challenges expectations and delights audiences with something they didn't realize they were longing for. *Once* is that musical."

—*Columbus Dispatch*

Once,

BOOKS BY ENDA WALSH
AVAILABLE FROM TCG

The New Electric Ballroom and *The Walworth Farce*

Once

Penelope

The Small Things and Other Plays
INCLUDES:
bedbound
Chatroom
Disco Pigs
The Ginger Ale Boy
How These Desperate Men Talk
Lynndie's Gotta Gun
misterman
The Small Things

BOOK

Enda Walsh

MUSIC AND LYRICS

Glen Hansard and Markéta Irglová

Based on the motion picture,
written and directed by John Carney

THEATRE COMMUNICATIONS GROUP
NEW YORK
2012

Once is published by Theatre Communications Group, Inc., 520 Eighth Avenue, 24th Floor, New York, NY 10018-4156, by special arrangement with Nick Hern Books Limited

The publication of *Once* by Enda Walsh, Glen Hansard and Markéta Irglová through TCG's Book Program, is made possible in part by the New York State Council on the Arts with the support of Governor Andrew Cuomo and the New York State Legislature.

TCG books are exclusively distributed to the book trade by Consortium Book Sales and Distribution.

Library of Congress Cataloging-in-Publication Data

Walsh, Enda.
Once / Book, Enda Walsh ; Music and Lyrics, Glen Hansard and Markéta Irglová. — First Edition.
pages cm
ISBN 978-1-55936-421-8
I. Hansard, Glen, 1970– composer. II. Irglová, Markéta, 1988– composer.
III. Title.
PR6123.A46O53   2012
822'.92—c23   2012039810

Book design and composition by Lisa Govan
Cover art by SpotCo

First Edition, December 2012

PREFACE

In April 2011 our production of *Once* was coming together in of all places—the basement of a church at Harvard!

The plan was to workshop the script there—to learn the music and songs—to get a sense of the staging and to perform in a small theater for a week and gauge what the hell we had. We were to do this in a packed three-week rehearsal period—in the basement of a church! (I mentioned that, right?) It should have been soul-destroying, exhausting work, but it really was the opposite.

I've never experienced such a creative environment before— such a positive rehearsal room. I used to turn up and sit there in awe of our director John Tiffany and movement director Steven Hoggett and watch as they whipped scenes out of thin air. Then our musical director Martin Lowe would floor me daily with his speed of thought, his amazingly concise direction and thunderous energy. I wanted to bottle the three of them up, freeze them and unleash them on my geriatric self some time in my sad future. I was lucky to be there. But I think we all felt that.

From the start it was always our idea to create an ensemble. It's something that's inherent in all theater productions of course but we wanted that to be our central philosophy. A cast of actors/musicians that would tell this delicate love story and would operate as a collective where one person can't work without the other—where the group is more powerful than the individual—where the alchemy of different instruments, different voices can hit the air and become something gorgeous.

It was an idea, a hope and somewhere in the casting—in the actors' decisions to put themselves forward—a quite extraordinary collection of individuals gathered. It was sort of divine and probably right that we were rehearsing below a church!

So we had each other, had a sweet love story that was finding its stage voice—and we had these songs.

I'm not musical—in that I can't play an instrument. I can belt out a song but it's not singing as such—it's more short bursts of vocalization that I call singing but it's not. Anyone who's seen my karaoke will vouch for that. I'm a "shouter." It's a mystery to me still how a song comes together. Story is my thing. I'm sure to many people writing a play is as baffling as songwriting is to me. But it's the frailty of a three-minute song—the concise honesty of that expression—that it happens so fully for such a short amount of time. That amazes me.

Glen and Markéta have carved out these powerful moments of honesty so completely. Whatever happened during the creation of these songs remains still. We understand that as a listener and as an audience. We know what it is to yearn for someone else, to lose a love, to feel unloved, to dream of an impossible union with someone else. They gave us these songs and we feel them wholly. Together with the film's director John Carney they made an unashamedly romantic love story—whose simplicity and power astounded me.

To develop this for the stage, with this ensemble of actors/musicians, has been a blessing for all involved.

The goal always is to make a true expression—to be one-hundred-percent honest with each other as makers—and to allow the characters to talk and speak as they would like.

So here are the songs—and here are the voices—and the extraordinary cast of *Once*. It has been the sweetest of journeys.

—Enda Walsh

once

PRODUCTION HISTORY

Once was originally developed at the American Repertory Theater (Diane Paulus, Artistic Director; Diane Borger, Producer) in Cambridge, Massachusetts, in April 2011. *Once* received its world premiere at New York Theatre Workshop (James C. Nicola, Artistic Director; William Russo, Managing Director) on November 15, 2011. It was directed by John Tiffany; set and costume design were by Bob Crowley, lighting design was by Natasha Katz, the sound design was by Clive Goodwin; the music supervisor and orchestrator was Martin Lowe; movement was by Steven Hoggett; the production stage manager was Bess Marie Glorioso. The cast was:

GUY	Steve Kazee
GIRL	Cristin Milioti
BILLY	Paul Whitty
DA	David Patrick Kelly
EX-GIRLFRIEND	Erikka Walsh
ŠVEC	Lucas Papaelias
ANDREJ	Will Connolly
RÉZA	Elizabeth A. Davis
BARUŠKA	Anne L. Nathan
IVANKA	Claire Candela
BANK MANAGER	Andy Taylor
EMCEE	J. Michael Zygo
EAMON	David Abeles

Once subsequently opened on Broadway at the Bernard B. Jacobs Theatre on March 18, 2012. It was produced by Robert Cole; Barbara Broccoli; John N. Hart, Jr.; Patrick Milling Smith; Frederick Zollo; Brian Carmody; Michael G. Wilson; Orin Wolf and The Shubert Organization, in association with New York Theatre Workshop. The cast and all personnel remained the same with the following exceptions: Ivanka was played alternately by Ripley Sobo and McKayla Twiggs.

CHARACTERS

GUY

GIRL

BILLY

DA

EX-GIRLFRIEND

ŠVEC

ANDREJ

RÉZA

BARUŠKA

IVANKA

BANK MANAGER

EMCEE

EAMON

LIST OF SONGS

THE SECOND HALF

When Your Mind's Made Up	*Guy, Girl, Ensemble*
Sleeping	*Guy*
The Hill	*Girl*
Gold (Reprise, a cappella)	*Billy, Ensemble*
The Moon (Reprise)	*Guy, Girl, Ensemble*
Falling Slowly (Reprise)	*Guy, Girl, Ensemble*

The first half.
As the audience takes its seat and waits in the auditorium, there's
a session on stage with musicians and singers belting out songs to one
another. It's raw, chaotic and hugely positive.
Suddenly it's dark and silent.
A light fades up on the Guy singing "Leave."

LEAVE

GUY:

> I can't wait forever is all that you said
> Before you stood up
> And you won't disappoint me
> I can do that myself
> But I'm glad that you've come
> Now if you don't mind
>
> Leave, leave,
> And free yourself at the same time
> Leave, leave,
> I don't understand, you've already gone

I hope you feel better
Now that it's out
What took you so long
And the truth has a habit
Of falling outta your mouth
Well now that it's come
If you don't mind

Leave, leave,
And please yourself at the same time
Leave, leave,
Let go of my hand
You said what you came to now
Leave, leave,
Let go of my hand
You said what you have to now
Leave, leave,
Leave, leave,
Let go of my hand
You said what you have to now
Leave, leave . . .

(He's finished.
He quietly takes the strap off the guitar and slowly lowers the
guitar to the ground.
He turns to leave the stage.
Then from the shadows:)

GIRL: That song you play—is it yours?

(He stops and looks into the darkness but can't see her just yet.)

I know you can talk I just heard you sing—unless you cannot
talk and only sing. If you want you can sing me your answer
to my question . . .
GUY *(He's leaving)*: No thanks.
GIRL: I made you talk just now.
GUY: I could talk already . . .
GIRL: So you write this song?
GUY: Yeah.

GIRL: It's very good.
GUY: Thanks.
GIRL: You're welcome. Hello.
GUY: Hey.

(A slight pause.)

GIRL: Is it always me who has to start the conversation?
GUY: Well you seem more up for it than I do.
GIRL: It's not even my language this English.
GUY: You speak it well.
GIRL: I have an accent.
GUY: We all have accents.
GIRL: We are people of the world.
GUY: Right.
GIRL: Do you enjoy being Irish?
GUY: Seriously?
GIRL: I'm always serious—I'm Czech. Are you enjoying your life right now?
GUY: Sorry, what?! . . .
GIRL: Why do you leave your guitar on the ground?
GUY: I don't want it anymore.
GIRL: Is it too heavy?
GUY: No.
GIRL: You should pick it up—guitars cost money.
GUY: Look I better go . . .
GIRL: Where?
GUY: To work.
GIRL: What is your work please?
GUY: I fix Hoovers.
GIRL: What is Hoovers?!
GUY: You know . . . vacuum cleaners.
GIRL: You fix vacuum cleaners?! My God, really?!!! This is incredible! I have here a vacuum cleaner that needs fixing.

(Somehow a vacuum cleaner has appeared right beside her.)

It was my destiny to meet you today—to listen to your beautiful song—to hear of your fabulous fixing.

GUY: Your destiny?

GIRL: It must be, right?!

GUY: So what's wrong with it?

GIRL: It doesn't suck. It's a Hoover without a suck. What could it be?

GUY: The motor or fan maybe . . .

GIRL: That's interesting.

GUY: Normal blockage in your pipes.

GIRL: Oh fascinating.

GUY: I'll need my tools to have a look.

GIRL: Your tools! My God, this is exciting! This day has such promise! Where is your shop?

GUY: Well it's my da's shop. I work with my da.

GIRL: You work with your da, ahh that's lovely.

GUY: Yeah it's really lovely.

(She hands him the Hoover and picks up his guitar.)

GIRL: You fix my Hoover I won't pay you with money, is this okay?

GUY: No money—right.

GIRL: I can pay you with music . . . if you like.

GUY: What do you play?

GIRL: My father teach me piano. He played violin with a big orchestra back home but then he gets arthritis—then he gets sad and then he kills himself. Before he go he teach me to play the piano. Piano is easier on the fingers than the violin.

GUY: Well that's good.

GIRL: I am still alive—I have yet to kill myself.

GUY: So I see.

GIRL: Five minutes ago you want to kill yourself but now I come to play you music and you to save my Hoover. Life is good, hey, even in Dublin.

GUY: I wasn't thinking of killing myself.

GIRL: Sure—only your guitar. But now I saved your guitar, too. We are saviors you and me, hah? So you fix my Hoover and I pay you with music, yes?

GUY: Do I have a choice?

GIRL: No.

(She holds out her hand. They shake on it.)

GUY: So you've got a piano?

GIRL: Oh a piano in Ireland is too expensive! I have nothing!

GUY: So where do you play?

(A piano is wheeled into the space by Billy.)

GIRL: A big man lets me play in his small shop. This is the small shop and this is the big man. His name is Billy.

BILLY: You're still talking to me, right? Not having you talk to me would kill me! Now about yesterday . . .

GIRL: We're grand.

BILLY: I just spoke out of turn. When you're a man of passion—passion can get the better of you—words spill out, you hear me?

GIRL: Yes.

BILLY: You're a beautiful girl—a woman—I'm a hot-blooded man.

GIRL: You're half Spanish.

BILLY: You remembered that! *(Pause)* I didn't mean to come on to you so heavy, is what I mean.

GIRL: You're grand . . .

BILLY: All I ever see is musos—grungy teenagers—rock star wannabes, who can't afford nothin'—but you! Look I'm sorry I said you had beautiful lips . . .

GIRL: This is a friend of mine.

(Billy turns quickly and suddenly sees the Guy for the first time. She goes to the piano—Billy goes to the Guy.)

BILLY: All right?

GUY: Yeah.

BILLY: Dubliner?

GUY: Yeah.

BILLY: Whereabouts?

GUY: Off the North Strand there.

BILLY: Northsider?

GUY: Yeah.

BILLY: Respect. Friend of hers then?

GUY: Just met her two minutes ago.

BILLY: Fucking lucky man! Fucking lucky!!

GIRL *(About the piano)*: So I can play this one, Billy?

BILLY: Of-course-love-yeah-absolutely-play-it! I'm closing up for lunch so just pull the door after ya, love.

(A slight pause. Billy moves closer to the Guy.)

I might have a chicken salad for my lunch actually.

GUY: Oh right?

BILLY: 'Cause despite the financial woes of this shop—I still look after myself from a dietry perspective.

GUY: Good man.

(Billy does an aggressive karate move at the Guy. He stops. He's pulled something.)

BILLY: Oh Jesus! ¡Adios camaradas!

(Billy turns away and leaves with a limp.)

GUY: Fucking hell!

GIRL: He's lovely, isn't he?

GUY: I thought he was going to kill me then.

GIRL: Yeah he's lovely.

GUY: He likes you he does.

GIRL: He's harmless—he just needs a sale.

(She hugs the piano.)

This is a beautiful piano. When I win the Lotto I will buy this piano and sleep with it every night. So first we say "hello" to it. *(Pause)* Hello!

(She looks at him and gestures him to speak.)

GUY *(To the piano)*: How's it goin'?

GIRL: This is serious. You must always say hello to the piano.

(He leans into the piano.)

GUY: Hello.

GIRL: Now how will I pay you? Bach, Bartók, Brahms, Mozart? Something of my own?

GUY: Whatever you like.

GIRL: Let's see.

(She settles herself and begins to play Mendelssohn's "Song without Words."
She completes it and stops.
A slight pause.)

GUY: Did you write that?

GIRL: No, Felix Mendelssohn did.

GUY: He's good isn't he?

GIRL: He's a romantic.

GUY: But dead right?

GIRL: He's a completely dead romantic. Now play me another song!

GUY: I don't want to sing anymore.

GIRL: Oh please! I pay you with money!

(She slaps a coin on the piano.)

GUY: Ten cent?!

GIRL: The size of the coin doesn't matter. You play or not play.

GUY: I wouldn't play if you handed me twenty Euro.

GIRL: I don't have ten Euro.

GUY: Well good 'cause I don't want to play anyway. Let's go!

GIRL: "Let's go"? We are in a music shop all alone and you sing very good songs—why are you giving up on your music?

GUY: There's no point to it anymore! It's got me nowhere!

GIRL: Because you are not Bono?

GUY: I don't want to be Bono!

GIRL: It has made you no money—you want to be famous?

GUY: You want to play your songs to people who want to listen!

GIRL: I am people! I want to listen! Play me a song!
GUY: Come on.

(He goes to leave. She grabs his bag. It falls onto the floor and sheet music spills out.
She's down quick, picking it up.)

GIRL: You write notes, too! You are like Mendelssohn—only alive—and Irish!
GUY: Can I have them back?!
GIRL: Music is dead to you! This is rubbish, right?!
GUY: Actually, yeah! Fuck it—keep it! Nice to have met ya!
GIRL: The transaction is not complete until you have made the Hoover suck!

(He turns back and looks at her.
He walks over and picks up the Hoover.
She starts to read and play the opening chords to "Falling Slowly."
He listens. She stops.)

Breathe. Are you breathing?
GUY: Yes I am.

(A slight pause.)

GIRL: You will not die if you play this song with me. *(Pause)* Please.

(Again she plays the opening to "Falling Slowly," and this time he accompanies her on his guitar and sings.)

FALLING SLOWLY

GUY:

> I don't know you
> But I want you
> All the more for that

(She begins to sing with him.)

GUY AND GIRL:
Words fall through me
And always fool me
And I can't react
And games that never amount

To more than they're meant
Will play themselves out

Take this sinking boat and point it home
We've still got time
Raise your hopeful voice you have a choice
You've made it now

Falling slowly, eyes that know me
And I can't go back
Moods that take me and erase me
And I'm painted black
You have suffered enough
And warred with yourself
It's time that you won

(The ensemble joins in, the song builds.)

Take this sinking boat and point it home
We've still got time
Raise your hopeful voice you have the choice
You've made it now

Falling slowly sing your melody
I'll sing it loud.

Take it all
I played the cards too late
Now it's gone.

(They finish.)

GIRL: So where is she?

GUY: Where's who?

GIRL: The girl in this song—is she dead?

GUY: No she's not dead—Jesus!

GIRL: So you still love her?

GUY: No we're finished.

GIRL: No one who writes this song is finished.

GUY: Well it's an old song.

GIRL: Your heart is not finished—I can hear in your voice. You sing this song to her and you will get her back.

GUY: Maybe I don't want her back.

GIRL: Maybe you are frightened to sing with such a big love?

GUY: Maybe I'm not bothered anymore.

GIRL: But maybe you should be bothered.

GUY: Right . . . *(Slight pause)* . . . well maybe we should go.

(She smiles.)

GIRL: To the North Strand.

GUY: The North Strand, yeah.

GIRL: I will take the guitar. Come on!

(They both leave.
"North Strand" is played with movement from the ensemble.
The Guy's elderly Da appears in the space, the other performers having dispersed as the music ends.
The Guy is seen working on the broken Hoover as a clock slowly ticks.
The Girl and Da sit together in silence. Finally:)

It's a fine shop you've got.

DA: Oh yeah?

(A slight pause.)

GIRL: Do you live above it?

DA: We do yeah. It's a little small up there but it's fine actually.

(A slight pause.)

GIRL: And just the two of you?

DA: Yeah. My wife died a year ago . . .

GIRL: Oh I'm sorry.

DA: Nah don't it's . . . ! *(Slight pause)* I couldn't live in the house after so. Sold up—moved upstairs here. I think it sort of suits me now.

GIRL: And you're doin' okay?

(A slight pause.)

DA: Yeah. Thank you.

(Da looks over at his son working.)

D'you think he's all right?

GIRL: I don't know. *(Slight pause)* He is maybe a little stopped?

DA: Right.

(A slight pause.)

He's a nice fella, mind you.

GIRL: Yes he is.

GUY: Well here ya go! I replaced the motor with something a little stronger.

GIRL: Great!

DA: Good lad.

GIRL: So what do I owe you?

GUY: Ya paid me with Mendelssohn, don't worry about it.

DA: With what?

GUY: Felix Mendelssohn, Da.

DA: And what's that?

GIRL: I'll pay you with money!

DA: Just give us five Euro, love.

GUY: Ah, Da . . .

GIRL: No it's grand.

DA: Friends rate. For friends.

GUY *(To himself)*: Jesus.

GIRL: Thank you, sir.

*(She hands Da five Euro in loose change and takes the Hoover. An
uncomfortable pause.)*

Well very nice to meet you.

DA: You're off then?

GIRL *(Looks to the Guy)*: Yeah I think our business is done . . .

DA: Maybe a bit of tea? A bite to eat?

GIRL: Nah I think I better . . .

GUY: Do you want to see my room?

(A pause.)

GIRL: What?

GUY: Just, you know, if you have a little time.

GIRL: Your bedroom?

GUY: If you want? *(Slight pause)* A cup of tea. Have a chat.

*(Da is suddenly gone.
    The Girl turns back to the Guy. She begins "The Moon":)*

THE MOON

GIRL:

> If you don't slow down, slow down
> If you don't slow down, slow . . .

Your room.

GUY: Yeah . . . pretty sad, isn't it?

GIRL: Yes.

(They sit as the song is being played.)

> Cut the bonds with the moon
> And let the dogs gather.

So you record all your music here?

GUY: Yeah—I got an old four-track and some other stuff, you
know but . . . I reckon I'm going to sell 'em now.

(The song finishes.)

GIRL: Nice song.

GUY: Thanks.

(Suddenly two voices can be heard. It's the Guy and his Ex-Girlfriend talking: her lines are spoken live; his are recorded.)

EX-GIRLFRIEND: It's really nice.

GUY: *You like it?*

(He runs to turn the four-track off.)

Right that's it!

GIRL: Is that her?! Leave it! I wanna hear her!

(She stops him.)

GUY: *Look tell me straight—I won't mind—you think it's all right?*

EX-GIRLFRIEND: It's beautiful.

GUY: *Honestly?*

EX-GIRLFRIEND: You're beautiful.

GUY: *Yeah sure.*

EX-GIRLFRIEND: Lie down, come on. Take your guitar off.

(Sound of them laughing.)

GUY: *Fuck I think we're still recording this.*

EX-GIRLFRIEND: Leave it on! Let's make our own single!

GUY: *Single my arse! Let's make a whole fucking album!*

(The Ex-Girlfriend laughs.
The recording stops itself.)

(Relieved) Oh thank Christ.

(A slight pause.)

GIRL: So when did she go?

GUY: Six months ago.

GIRL: And where?

GUY: To New York. Nothin' really for her here—no job, no prospects . . .

GIRL: Just you?

GUY: Yeah.

GIRL: And your music.

GUY: I speak to her on the phone sometimes.

GIRL: And how is she?

GUY: Oh she was lonely at the start, I think—but she's met someone new now so . . .

GIRL: Why don't you kill him?

GUY *(Smiling)*: Kill him, of course.

GIRL: I can help you. I can get a gun from this man.

GUY: What seriously?

GIRL: Yeah. I'm always serious—I'm Czech.

GUY *(Laughing)*: Oh fuck!

GIRL: He's just a passing guy for her—I can tell. You should go to New York—you're living in a little boy's room.

GUY: My da needs the help.

GIRL: You are going to stay here, fixing Hoovers and living over a shop forever?!

GUY: Well not "forever" . . .

GIRL: Go to New York, find your woman, sing your songs to people!

GUY: Just like that?!

GIRL: Why not?

GUY: I could barely afford the ticket even if I wanted to go all that way and stalk a woman who's getting on fine without me! And the music?! . . . No one wants to hear it! It's easier to walk away from it!

GIRL: I won't allow you do that!

(A slight pause.)

GUY: Why won't you allow me?

(A pause.)

GIRL: Can you make a CD so I can listen to more of your songs?

GUY: If you want, yeah.

GIRL: We can meet tomorrow again and talk maybe? I gotta go now.

GUY: What's the rush?

GIRL: I need to go.

GUY: Oh come on, stay!

GIRL: What do you mean "stay"?

GUY: Well why don't you stay the night?

(A slight pause.)

GIRL: And "make a whole album"?

(A slight pause.)

GUY: Or maybe just a few singles.

(He goes in for a kiss but she grabs his face in her hand.)

GIRL *(She's hurt)*: Fuck you.

(The Girl leaves the space.
He cringes. What an asshole.
He walks across the stage and sings:)

THE MOON

GUY:

    If you don't slow down, slow down
    If you don't slow down, slow . . .

(He walks into Billy's shop and turns on the Hoover.
Billy and the Girl look up at him. The Guy turns it off.)

Can I have a moment, Billy?

BILLY: Yeah-sure-a-moment-absolutely-for-what?!

GUY: Just a quiet word . . .

GIRL: Say it.

BILLY: Yeah say it! No secrets between me and her. Right, love?

GIRL: Right, pal.

(Billy and the Girl do an elaborate handshake. They stop and face the Guy.)

GUY: Right. *(Slight pause)* Look I'm sorry I made a pass at ya yesterday.

BILLY: You did what?!

GUY: I'm a bit lonely . . .

BILLY: We're all a bit lonely! Lonely's a big part of the world these days! But you learn restraint, d'you hear me!

GUY: Yeah of course . . .

BILLY: You'd have to be a corpse not to feel some attraction for this angel of divinity . . .

GUY: I know . . .

BILLY: Which makes the restraint all the more problematic! But you do it because . . .

GIRL: Because it's against the law to force yourself on a woman.

BILLY: Exactly! *(To the Guy)* Did you force yourself on her?!

GUY: No! Jesus! I didn't, did I?

BILLY: How could you forget?!

GUY: I definitely didn't!

BILLY: I can do karate! You know that, right?!

GUY: Yeah I saw.

BILLY: These are lethal weapons these! I take it on myself to protect the unprotected! I could slice you into pieces and rearrange ya back together again but fuck you up for life, comprende?!

GUY: Of course yeah!!

(A pause.)

BILLY: All right, we're all cool here. We're not going to have a *CSI* situation in me shop. You've accepted his apology, is that right, love?

GIRL: Yeah we're grand—yeah.

(The Guy and the Girl shake hands.
Billy pulls the Guy aside and has a final quiet word:)

BILLY: You have to learn a little more reserve, yeah?—a rush of blood to your head, you count to ten and take a shower, all right?

GUY: A shower, okay.

BILLY: If a shower's not available at the time—listen to some Josh Groban—that usually takes the edge off me anyways. Buddies?

GUY: Cool-Billy-yeah.

(Billy gives the Guy a "friendly" punch on the shoulder.
The Guy turns back to the Girl, and they're suddenly in a different lighting state.)

GIRL: Thank you for walking me home.

GUY: I reckon if I didn't Billy would have sliced me to pieces—so just lookin' after myself really.

(She smiles.)

Oh look I burnt you some songs! *(He hands her a CD)*

GIRL: Oh great!

GUY: The quality's not all that but . . . well if you ever fancy listening . . .

GIRL: I will—I want to.

GUY: Thanks for being interested by the way.

GIRL: Sure.

(A long pause. He really doesn't want to say good-bye. Then:)

Do you want to come in for a cup of tea?

GUY: Yeah. I'd love to!

(A new lighting state: the Girl and the Guy enter a whirlwind of a scene.
Her flatmates, two men: Švec; Andrej, in a fast food uniform; and a young heavily "makeup-ed" woman, Réza, are discussing passionately the Irish television soap Fair City.

*The Girl's formidable-looking mother, Baruška, files her nails
and looks on.*

*They speak in English, but Czech is shown on surtitles behind
them.)*

ANDREJ: She's a liar—the woman is evil!

GIRL: These are my flatmates.

GUY: You all live here?

GIRL: Yes it's very cozy.

RÉZA: She's not evil! You're an idiot!

ANDREJ: How can Damien lie in the same bed as that witch?!

GUY: Is everything all right?

ANDREJ: The deceit! My God!!

GIRL: They're talking about *Fair City.*

GUY: The soap opera?

RÉZA: You understand nothing! Don't you live in the world?!
This is the real world, Andrej!

ŠVEC: But Suzanne is changing.

GIRL: They learn their English from the soaps on television. *Fair
City* is their passion.

ŠVEC: Can you see what they're doing with Suzanne's looks?

ANDREJ: Suzanne promised, Réza! She swore on her life! She's
the devil!

GIRL: Speak English!

(The surtitles disappear as they speak English.)

ANDREJ: She beats her own husband and then she promised that
she would see a counselor! Suzanne lied that she was seeing
this counselor!

RÉZA: Damien is a worm!

ANDREJ: Damien is a man who watched his own father kill his
own mother! And now to be suffering abuse at the hands of
his own fucking wife!

ŠVEC: But they're making her more attractive the more violent
she gets. Have you noticed that? It's very clever.

ANDREJ: You think she's more attractive, Švec?

ŠVEC: Definitely!

ANDREJ: Her domestic abuse is turning you on?!

ŠVEC: Suzanne is a ride.

ANDREJ: You are a pervert!

ŠVEC: Oh yes.

ANDREJ *(Noticing the Guy)*: Who are you?

(A slight pause.)

GUY: No one.

ANDREJ: Do not look at my uniform with disgust. Today I am the manager. In two days I will interview and I will be the area manager. I will oversee the creation and distribution of fine foods to the lovely people of Dublin.

GUY: Fair play.

RÉZA: Where d'you pick him up?

GIRL: The street.

RÉZA: Is he single?

GIRL: Leave him alone.

RÉZA: So Irishman . . . you are very handsome.

GUY: Thank you.

RÉZA: For an Irishman you are handsome. I am looking for an Irish husband, actually. An animal—but a sensitive animal. Do you know of such an animal?

ŠVEC: Hey, Irish. *(A fierce Dublin accent)* "Fancy a pint in McCoy's later, yeah bud?" "What d'you mean you're pregnant?! Jaysus dats awful news!" "I'm keepin' da baby! I want ta keep da baby!"

(A slight pause.)

GUY: Very good.

ŠVEC: Tank you.

GUY: Great accent.

ŠVEC: Deadly, isn't it?!

GIRL: This is my mother, Baruška.

(Baruška walks toward him, grabs the Guy and kisses him full on the lips.
The kiss breaks and she stares at him.)

BARUŠKA: Jist?!

(A slight pause.)

GUY: What does "Jist" mean?

GIRL: Eat.

GUY: She wants to eat me?

BARUŠKA *(In English)*: You eat my food, yes?!

GUY: "Eat your food"? Excellent!

(A little five-year-old girl, dressed in her pajamas, Ivanka, has walked on stage and stands behind the Guy. She tugs at his jumper. He turns and looks down at her.)

GIRL: This is my daughter Ivanka.

GUY: Hey there.

(Ivanka holds out her hand. They shake hands.)

EJ PADÁ, PADÁ ROSIČKA

BARUŠKA: ZPÍVAT!

Ej padá, padá rosička

Eh pa da, pa da row sich ka
Eh pa da, pa da row sich ka
Eh pa da, pa da row sich ka

Spa lee bi moh yeh oh cheech kah
Spa lee bi moh yeh
Spa lee bee ye tvoh yeh
Spa lee bi oh nee oh bow yeh
Hey hey hey hey hey hey hey hey

Eye pur shi pur shi na poh zjrad
Skash teh poz dra vit nap o zjrad
Skash teh poz drau e nee
Me moo poh tye shen dee

Zjeh oozh ho moo seem zah nech at
Eye pur shi pur shi na poh zjrad

Skash teh poz dra vit na po zjrad
Skash teh poz drau e nee
Me moo poh tye shen dee

Zjeh oozh ho moo seem zah nech at

Hey hey hey hey hey hey hey hey.

*(Andrej and Réza dance on the table throughout. The flat is going
wild. The Guy is standing back smiling.*
The song, dancing and dinner come to an end.
A new lighting state with only the Guy and Girl sitting in it.
She's wearing large headphones and listening to his CD.)

GIRL *(Shouting)*: This is just music! Where's the words?
GUY: There are none.
GIRL *(Shouting)*: It's great! You've no words for this?!
GUY: Got a few ideas . . .
GIRL *(Shouting)*: Hah?

(He lifts the headphones off her ears.)

GUY: I couldn't settle on the lyrics. You can try some if you fancy
    it.
GIRL: Really?
GUY: Yeah if you want.
GIRL: Okay. *(Slight pause)* This is romantic. You have a romantic
    streak.
GUY: I used to.
GIRL: When?
GUY: When I was younger.
GIRL: But now you are an old man.

(He smiles.)

GUY: So where is Ivanka's da?

GIRL: He doesn't live here.

(A slight pause.)

GUY: Why's that?
GIRL: It's difficult between us. He's at home now.

(A pause.)

Thank you for the Hoover . . . and for the songs.
GUY: Thanks for the company. I really needed it.
GIRL: Me, too.

(A pause. He would love to stay.)

Oh! Take your guitar. Come on.

(He takes the guitar.)

I will see you tomorrow?
GUY: Where?
GIRL: I'll find you.

(He walks out of the light.
She sits for a number of seconds looking in the direction from
where he left.
Baruška appears with Ivanka.)

BARUŠKA: He is a nice man.
GIRL: We're just friends—
BARUŠKA: Of course.
GIRL: —that's all . . .
BARUŠKA: I can see.

(A pause.)

GIRL: His life's stopped. But he has a good heart.
BARUŠKA: And you? *(Slight pause)* You're not stopped, too?

(A pause.)

Your man—he left you here . . . *(Slight pause)* —now you can
start over.

GIRL: Don't say that—

BARUŠKA: It's true.

GIRL: It's not a simple thing, Mama!

BARUŠKA: I know . . .

GIRL: Good night.

(A slight pause. The conversation's over.)

BARUŠKA: Good night, love.

(Baruška kisses her and leaves the light.
With Ivanka sleeping beside her, the Girl looks down at the
CD player. She presses the play button and the ensemble plays "If
You Want Me" as she sings:)

IF YOU WANT ME

GIRL:

Are you really here or am I dreaming
I can't tell dreams from truth
For it's been so long since I have seen you
I can hardly remember your face anymore
When I get really lonely and the distance causes only
    silence
I think of you smiling with pride in your eyes a lover
    that sighs

If you want me satisfy me
If you want me satisfy me
Are you really sure that you believe me
When others say I lie
I wonder if you could ever despise me
When you know I really tried
To be a better one to satisfy you for you're everything
    to me

And I'll do what you ask me
If you let me be free

If you want me satisfy me
If you want me satisfy me
If you want me satisfy me
If you want me satisfy me.

(The music continues.
The Girl picks up Ivanka and carries her out of the light.
The music ends.
New lighting state.
The Guy is facing a mirror. He's singing and strumming an
improvised biographical song. The Girl remains unseen by him.)

BROKEN-HEARTED HOOVER FIXER SUCKER GUY

GUY:

Ten years ago
I fell in love with an Irish girl
She took my heart

But she went and screwed some guy that she knew
And now I'm in Dublin with a broken heart

Oh broken-hearted Hoover fixer sucker guy
Oh broken-hearted Hoover fixer sucker sucker guy

One day I'll go there and win her once again
But until then I'm just a sucker of a guy.

(He turns and sees the Girl. He visibly blushes.)

Hey.

GIRL: Hey. I listen to all your songs and I have made a big deci-
sion. Do you want to hear it?

GUY: Would love ta.

GIRL: You write these songs for your girl and now she is gone these songs have made you depressed. But they have heart and soul and you have heart and soul. These songs they need to be sung for you, for me, for anyone who has lost a love. Don't be sad—you must sing.

GUY: I know.

GIRL: You know? I am going to hug you right now.

GUY: Fair enough.

(The Girl hugs him. She stops and holds him back.)

GIRL: So we are going to make a demonstration tape of these songs—me and you—with good musicians—and we send this tape around the world and a fat man with a fat cigar will pick you up for his record company and you will go to New York and you make something of yourself, okay?!

GUY: Okay . . .

GIRL: So I speak to a man today in a recording studio and I bash him down in price and we can have his studio for twenty-four hours. One day—two grand!

GUY: Where would I find two grand?!

GIRL: My mother borrow money from the small loans man in the bank and this man is a nice and a good man. My mother pay this man back so we are in the good books.

GUY: All right.

GIRL: Now you dress like a tramp—

(She whips a gray shiny suit out of a plastic bag.)

Take your clothes off!

(He starts taking off his trousers.)

GUY: Did you buy that?!

GIRL: It is a suit from Andrej. It is a great suit. His lucky interview suit. A suit to impress the bank man.

GUY: Well I better get these trousers on—I don't want to drive ya wild!

GIRL: No—your naked legs would make me explode.

GUY: Where do you get your energy from?
GIRL: I am a young mother. We are a special breed.

(He gets the trousers on.)

GUY: Done.

*(She turns and looks at him in the suit.
A quiet moment as she straightens and buttons his jacket. Then:)*

GIRL: Let's go!

*(He grabs his guitar.
Music is played as the ensemble arrives on stage with seats.
They sit in rows and suddenly we're in the open-plan office of the
bank.
At the front of the stage the Bank Manager is waiting.
The Guy and the Girl enter the space. Suddenly he's nervous.
Baruška stops them.)*

BARUŠKA *(To the Guy, referring to the Girl)*: She will translate.
GUY: Okay.

*(Baruška speaks in English, her words appearing in Czech sur-
titles.)*

BARUŠKA: Once upon a time there was a little man who lived
in a little house in a little city and he had a little job in a
little office—and nothing ever happened to this little man.
In truth he was a miserable little man. And one night he lay
awake in his bed and for the first time in his life he imagined
great adventures. He imagined other countries and fantastic encounters with unstable individuals. He imagined love
affairs of various varieties. He slept deeply and what great
dreams he had! The morning came and he dressed—but
not in the clothes he would usually wear—this morning he
would be brand new! But then . . . as he faced his front door
to the world outside he closed his eyes and that same mind
began to imagine the most terrible things. Instead where

before he only saw life and success—now he only saw death and failure. The world outside was there to torture and crush him! Love was there to tease and break him! FUCK IT! He stripped out of his new clothes, returned to his bed and promised never to dream of anything ever again. He remained in that bed for eternity, emaciated and rotting, lying in his own shit, his one expression he gave to the world crawled from his mouth . . .

(Baruška does the tortured choking sound of "the emaciated failure." She stops.)

(To the Guy, in Czech) "Those who live in fear . . . die miserably in their graves."

(The Guy is shook to his core. He turns to the Girl.)

GUY: So what did she say?

(A slight pause.)

GIRL: Good luck.

(The Guy and the Girl leave Baruška. They enter the bank and walk through the "secretaries."
They are met by the Bank Manager. The three sit as the Bank Manager looks at their written application.
The Bank Manager's a prim man from County Cork.)

BANK MANAGER: I can't say I see many applications like this one—a bit out of the norm for me. So you've never held an account in this bank?
GUY: No.
BANK MANAGER: In any bank?
GUY: I've got a post office account.
BANK MANAGER: Oh terrific.
GUY: My da says postmen are a lot more honest than bankers.
BANK MANAGER: Does he now?
GUY: He does yeah.

GIRL: He is a very good song writer, sir.

BANK MANAGER: Lovely . . .

GIRL: We will pay you back with interest when we get the deal.

BANK MANAGER: Well that's how it works, you see! I give you the loan and you repay me with interest which won't be a problem because you're going to be snapped up and handed a ferociously large record contract by a major record company.

GIRL *(A little nervous)*: Can I ask you a question?

BANK MANAGER: Yeah why not!

GIRL: Are you proud to be Irish?

BANK MANAGER: Well that's a very personal question.

GIRL: Are you proud or not proud? It is not difficult.

BANK MANAGER: Fundamentally I am proud, I suppose.

GIRL: And what makes you the most proud? The first thing.

BANK MANAGER *(Immediately)*: Our culture.

GIRL: For an island this tiny to make all these writers and poets and musicians! This is insane. And yet on this little rock in the middle of the ocean you make men and women who for centuries can speak and sing of what it is to be a person. Yeats, Swift, Wilde, Beckett, Joyce, Van Morrison, Enya, the fantastic people who gave the world Riverdance! But it is people like you! People who invest in Irish culture who also make the culture, sir! You are responsible for showing the world that Ireland is still here! Ireland is open for business!

(A slight pause.)

BANK MANAGER: Very good.

GIRL: Thank you.

BANK MANAGER: Very impressive.

GIRL: And the loan?

BANK MANAGER: Listen I'm sorry but I'd need some real assurance of recuperation if I was to bring this any further . . .

GIRL *(To the Guy)*: Play!

(The Guy begins to play "Say It to Me Now.")

BANK MANAGER: It's true there are countless people in Ireland that need financial assistance right now . . .

GIRL: Keep playing!

BANK MANAGER: . . . And I'm sure you're talented and everything . . . you can certainly memorize musical chords and play them in a melodic sequence . . . but really . . .

GIRL: Sing!

(The Guy sings.)

SAY IT TO ME NOW

GUY:

I'm scratching at the surface now

(The Bank Manager doesn't know what to do . . . but listen.)

And I'm trying hard to work it out
So much has gone misunderstood
This mystery only leads to doubt.

And I'm looking for a sign
And this a dark and uneasy time
If you have something to say
You'd better say it now

'Cause this is what you've waited for
Your chance to even up the score
And as these shadows fall on me now
I will somehow

'Cause I'm picking up a message, Lord
And I'm closer than I've ever been before

So if you have something to say
Say it to me now
Say it to me now . . .

(A pause.
The Bank Manager is blown away.)

BANK MANAGER: Do you have many more like that?
GIRL: Very many.
BANK MANAGER: Great voice. Really good.
GUY: Thanks.
BANK MANAGER: Raw.
GUY: I suppose, yeah.
BANK MANAGER: What sort of guitar is that?
GUY: An old Martin.
BANK MANAGER: Oh lovely! *(Pause)* Can I show you something?
GUY: Yeah sure.

(He turns and grabs a beautiful guitar.)

BANK MANAGER: Feast your eyes on this baby.
GUY: Amazing.
BANK MANAGER: Should be—cost me an arm and a leg! Now I'm going to play you two a little something. It's my own cultural crusade if you like but I want your honest opinion, okay?
GIRL: I am all about honesty.
GUY: She is the Ambassador of Honesty.
BANK MANAGER: Great stuff! Now by way of introduction . . .
GIRL: Play!
BANK MANAGER: It's a work in progress . . .
GIRL: Play!
BANK MANAGER: Some important biographical decisions to make . . .
GIRL: Play!

*(The Bank Manager launches into his own composition.
It's a country western song called "Abandoned in Bandon.")*

ABANDONED IN BANDON

BANK MANAGER:
In County Cork in the country green,
In a lonesome town called Bandon.
A boy lives there and he dreams of County Clare
The holiday that he just had done.

And he walked over hills and skipped over rivers,
All the time his hand in his love.
But his love's not here and never close at hand
His heart's abandoned in Bandon.

Two counties. One love.
Too many complications
And not enough hand in glove.

Not enough hand in glove.

(The Guy and Girl sit frozen with strained smiles on their faces.)

Took a drive outta town an' kept on drivin',
His Western love—his navigation.
But the car broke down outside of Castletown,
He pulled into the gas station.

He dialed that name and imagined them kissin',
As that sweet Clare voice filled his ears,
But his love's not here and never close at hand.
His car's all bust 'cause he bust the gears.

Two counties. One love.
Too many complications
And not enough hand in glove.
Not enough hand in glove.

Abandoned in Bandon.

(He finishes. The Guy and Girl are rightly stunned.
He quietly takes off his guitar and holds it out.
A pause.)

Well?
GUY: You can play.
BANK MANAGER: Yeah.

(The Guy and Bank Manager look to the Girl.)

GIRL: It's the voice—and the words.
GUY: Never sing.
GIRL: Ever.
BANK MANAGER: Understood. Thank you.
GIRL: Sure.

(A pause. He looks like he's really going to cry. The Guy and Girl cringe. Maybe that was the wrong thing to do. But then:)

BANK MANAGER: So how much money are we talking about?

(A dramatic light change with loud music. We're in a pub. In a spotlight Réza is performing a dance track Shakira-style. The Guy and the Girl are out celebrating their success with Andrej and Švec.)

GUY: How long have I known ya?
GIRL: Two days, six hours, *(She checks her watch)* thirty-five minutes.
GUY: I don't really get it.
GIRL: What don't you get?
GUY: Well you've been so kind an' everything—given me a new me! I don't know how to thank ya!
GIRL: Let's sit down . . .
GUY: No hang on! *(Slight pause)* Listen when we met I was in a bad place—it was more than giving up on music and you knew that. I love my da more than the world but my little room above the shop and the same view of the street outside—that was looking like my life forever. *(Slight pause)* And that was only two days ago. Two days. *(Slight pause)* So thank you.
EMCEE: Let's hear it for Réza. Next up on the Live Mike we got the Hooverman!

(The ensemble cheers and jeers throughout the below.)

GIRL: It's you!
GUY: What's me?!
EMCEE: Come on the Hooverman!

GUY: You put me down to sing?!

GIRL: You must get used to singing your songs on stage, right?!

GUY: Oh Jaysus! . . .

(Some of the crowd begins to chant "Hoover!"
A spotlight comes up on the Guy.)

EMCEE: The Hooverman! This guy's gonna suck!

(There's cheering as the Guy walks up and steps behind the micro-
phone. He's bloody nervous up there.)

ANDREJ: Hey, Hoover! Nice suit!

(Nothing.)

GUY: Well this is a song that I wrote . . .

VOICE 1: Ahh fuck!

VOICE 2: He wrote it?!

(A slight pause.)

GUY: Yeah I wrote it for a girl but eh . . . But tonight I'd like to sing it now for—

VOICE 3: A boy!

GUY: . . . well for all of us here. 'Cause to live . . . you have to love.

VOICE 4: Sweet Jesus.

(People laugh. The Guy begins to sing "Gold.")

GOLD

GUY:

> And I love her so
> I wouldn't trade her for gold
> I'm walking on moonbeams
> I was born with a silver spoon

And I'm gonna be me
I'm gonna be free
I'm walking on moonbeams
and staring out to sea

And if a door be closed
Then a row of homes start building
And tear your curtains down
For sunlight is like gold

*(The Girl is seen standing looking at him. We focus on her more
and more, as if they are the only two on stage.)*

And you better be you
And do what you can do

When you're walking on moonbeams
Staring out to sea

'Cause if your skin was soil
How long do you think before they start digging?

And if your life was gold
How long do you think you'd stay livin'?
Hey . . .

(He smiles down at her, she smiles back.
But there's a moment suddenly in her heart, a huge worry.)

And I love her so
I wouldn't trade her for gold.

(She's fallen in love with him.
Fade out. Blackout.
Interval.)

ENDA WALSH, GLEN HANSARD AND MARKÉTA IRGLOVÁ

The second half.

A short musical introduction—and suddenly the light comes up in Billy's shop with Billy, the Bank Manager, Švec, Andrej (in the gray suit) and the Guy and the Girl. The atmosphere is immediately strained.

BILLY: Now wait a second—you're absolutely joking me—let me get this straight—you're a banker, is that right?

BANK MANAGER: You've heard it three times now!

BILLY: The very people who are threatening to steal these premises offa me if I don't start making sales! A banker from Cork—am I the only person who's uncomfortable with this?

GIRL: Yes! Let's rehearse!

ANDREJ *(To the Bank Manager)*: I have not been placed on this world to flip burgers! I am a builder of worlds. This is a lucky suit! Today I am the manager. In two hours I will interview and I will be the area manager!

BANK MANAGER: Fair play.

ANDREJ: You are looking at the last moments of a burger-boy. This is a great day for Andrej!

BILLY: It's the combination of Cork and banker, am I right?!

BANK MANAGER: And what's wrong with Cork?!

ŠVEC *(In his Dublin accent)*: Cork is a dump!

BILLY: Exactly! Nice accent.

ŠVEC: I learn me English offa *Fair City*.

BILLY: Suzanne's looking great isn't she—the more psycho she's gettin'?

ŠVEC: Suzanne's a ride, man!

ANDREJ: Suzanne is a monster!

BANK MANAGER: Suzanne is mental!

BILLY *(To the Bank Manager)*: You still here, Corkman?

GIRL: Billy, stop!

BILLY: My shop—my rules! The establishment is not welcome here, love! We are creators of music. We are free of the shackles of capitalism!

GUY: You own a shop, Billy!

BILLY: That's true—but I've got the heart of an artist! *(To the Bank Manager)* Now fuck off!

BANK MANAGER: I am as much an artist as you are! That man is an ignorant fecker!

BILLY: I might very well be an ignorant fecker—but at least I'm a Dublin one!

ŠVEC: And Dublin's deadly man!

BILLY: As my Dublin friend says!

BANK MANAGER: He's Czech!

GIRL: SHUT UP!

(Silence.)

For a few moments just keep the shit-talk inside yourselves! Billy?

(A slight pause.)

BILLY: For the sake of rehearsal and my commitment to this musical odyssey I will suspend my instinct and channel my energies into the melody.

(The Girl looks at the Bank Manager.)

BANK MANAGER: For the sake of my investment—let's play.

BILLY *(Hardly under his breath)*: Wanker.

(The Girl fires a look at him.)

ŠVEC: Very nice drums this.

BILLY: Thanks.

GUY: You've played drums before, right?

ŠVEC: I played in a music group back home.

GUY: Oh cool!

ŠVEC: A death metal band. I play hard.

GUY: Well this might be a little more folksy than metal.

ŠVEC: Folksy?

GUY: Can you play softer?

ŠVEC: I will muffle the drums.

GUY: With what?

ŠVEC *(Quickly ripping off his trousers to shorts)*: Pants, man! My PANTS!!

GIRL: Are we ready?

GUY: Yeah. Let's give it a lash. This is the chorus. It's in A-minor.

(They begin to play "When Your Mind's Made Up." Švec is on drums, the Bank Manager is on cello, Andrej's on double bass, Billy's on guitar, the Girl is on piano and the Guy on rhythm guitar. The Guy and Girl start well but when the others join in they all start competing with each other.
It's soon a discordant mess. It collapses with:)

Ahh, Jaysus!

GIRL *(To Billy)*: What are you playing?! What was that?!

BILLY: It needs to travel a little more—it's very sleepy!

ŠVEC: More soul—less pants!

ANDREJ: A bit more swing definitely.

GIRL: No fancy stuff!

BANK MANAGER: We need to express something!

BILLY: Express yourself outta here—you're brutal!

GUY: Hoy!

BILLY: You're crap!

BANK MANAGER: A fish could play better guitar than you!

BILLY: Get outta Dublin ya big Cork eegit! Ya make me sick! Your accent makes me sicker!

BANK MANAGER: I'm leaving!

BILLY: YOU STAY RIGHT THERE YOU CARPETBAG-
GER! It's me who owns you, Banker—it's me who's walkin'
out! You can take your fucking cello and shove it up your
arsehole! It's finished!

(Billy leaves. The others are stunned, devastated.
A long pause.
Billy returns.)

Obviously this is my shop and it's you who'll have to leave.
BANK MANAGER: Obviously.
BILLY: Rehearsal's over! All of ya . . . get out!

(A new lighting state.
We're in a noisy pub with Billy and the Guy.)

GUY: I need ya, Billy—I need ya big time!
BILLY: I hate that banker! They're crushin' me into the ground—
I'm a man of principle—I can't do it! I'm out!
GUY: I'm beggin' ya, please!
BILLY: Don't beg me!
GUY: Well I don't wanna beg ya!
BILLY: Flatter me then!
GUY: Flatter ya?
BILLY: I need it!! *(Slight pause)* Flatter me.

(A slight pause.)

GUY: You're a beautiful man.

(A slight pause.)

BILLY: Yeah I do have a beauty.
GUY: You've got a real feel for the music too—I can tell, Billy.
BILLY: You reckon?
GUY: Oh definitely! I need your playin'!
BILLY: You think I play good?!
GUY: You play massive, man! Massive!
BILLY: This is helpin' me! I'm feelin' better! Get me a drink.

GUY: Anything at all—the bar's yours.
BILLY: A glass of rioja.

(The light flicks off them and onto the Girl and Réza on the other side of the bar.)

GIRL: We need Billy—we need his drums.

(A slight pause.)

RÉZA: What's it worth?
GIRL: I need it as a favor.
RÉZA: You want me to seduce this man I will need payment.
GIRL: You seduce men for fun!
RÉZA: With this one I will need encouragement—get me a drink.
GIRL: What do you want?
RÉZA: A whiskey. A double.

(The light flicks off them and back on Billy and the Guy.)

BILLY: D'you want an observation?
GUY: Not really.
BILLY: She likes you.
GUY: Right.
BILLY: I have an intuition about these things.
GUY: I don't wanna talk about it . . .
BILLY: Over a year I've worked on unlocking her heart and not even a lookin'! You waltz in and BAM! You're a love thief— but I respect you for that. Now what are you going to do about it?
GUY: I don't want to talk about this with you!
BILLY: We are talking about this!
GUY: LOOK WE NEED YOUR DRUMS!
BILLY: DRUMS?! I thought you wanted me for my "massive" playing! YA SNAKE!

(The light flicks off them and back on Réza and the Girl.)

RÉZA: Now pay me with honesty.

GIRL: What do you want to know?

RÉZA: This very attractive man with the dark looks and wide shoulders—

GIRL: Yes I know who you're talking about.

RÉZA: Do you want him?

GIRL: In the way that you want him?

(A slight pause.)

RÉZA: Do you want to be with him?

GIRL: I am with someone.

RÉZA: With someone who can't see how beautiful you are! This man is sweet. He has the same soul as you.

GIRL: He is going to America to be with his girl.

RÉZA: You're standing in front of him!

GIRL: Réza please!

RÉZA: Do it for you!

GIRL: It's not important right now!

RÉZA: What could be more important than love?!

GIRL: Drums! We need Billy's drums! Please!

(Réza knocks back her whiskey.
The Girl turns Réza, then shoves her toward Billy, who stands at the bar.
Réza taps him on the shoulder, he turns.)

RÉZA: So, Irishman—you drink red wine?

BILLY: In 1588 my Spanish ancestor stepped on to the Irish coast off his colossal sea vessel. With me—it's always rioja.

RÉZA: They say a man who drinks rioja is a bull in the bed.

BILLY: A bull in the sheets—a butterfly on the dance floor.

(A blast of Latin dance music and Billy strikes a Flamenco pose.)

RÉZA: Fabuloso!

(Réza and Billy dance. Billy throws his back out. Réza helps him off.
Suddenly Andrej runs into the space screaming and drunk. He rips off his lucky jacket and throws it on the ground.)

ENDA WALSH, GLEN HANSARD AND MARKÉTA IRGLOVÁ

ANDREJ (*Screams*): Bastards! The bastards! Bastards . . .

> (*He cries for some time, his dream of being area manager crushed.*
> *The others can only look on.*)

GUY: Oh fuck it!

GIRL: Don't worry. Réza will get Billy. She is a tough woman.

GUY: But everything else. Not even gettin' started and it's falling apart—it's typical . . .

GIRL: Stop.

> (*A slight pause.*)

GUY: Let's do something. Get out of the city and breathe a little.

GIRL: I should go.

GUY: Please.

> (*A pause.*)

GIRL: Okay.

> (*A transition here as the Guy and Girl enter a new state.*
> *They look over Dublin from Howth Head. Sound of the sea.*)

GUY: What's the Czech for ocean?

GIRL: "Ocean." (*Slight pause*) It's the same.

GUY: Really?

GIRL: Yeah.

> (*A slight pause.*)

GUY: Easy language, isn't it?

GIRL: Yeah it's very easy.

GUY: No point having it really.

GIRL: No.

> (*A pause.*)

Look at the little lights. The city looks tiny from here.

GUY: It does. It is.

(A pause.)

Does Dublin feel like home?

GIRL: I think so. It never became what it wanted to be . . . but it's still a life and a good one I think. Very good people. Big-hearted people.

GUY: That'll be all those potatoes.

(She laughs.)

GIRL: You'll miss it when you go to New York.

GUY: I suppose.

(A pause.)

GIRL: It's so nice here.

GUY: Yeah.

(A slight pause.)

I used to come here as a boy on the good Sundays when the weather wasn't crap—me, Ma and Da on the train. It was great. Twenty-minute train journey but it may as well have been Borneo or somethin'.

(A slight pause.)

My ma brought me with two of my friends once. And we were walkin' the cliff walk way down there. And, ya know, like boys we were messin' about, gettin' a little bit too close to the edge. And I think we must have wandered off the path, gone a bit lower and onto a smaller, narrower path—and there's this big rock juttin' out blockin' us and beyond the rock the path is much wider and safer definitely. We're all only about seven years old and my ma can easily lift us over the rock and back onto the path, and one by one she does that. *(Slight pause)* So I'm on the safe side and watching her climb over the rock on her own. She's holding on to it and her little flat shoes are finding a grip. *(Slight pause)* I look down, and way below is a terrible fall and sharp rocks and ocean. And I start crying. *(Slight pause)* And of course she makes it to the other side and the rest of the day is all fish and chips and ice cream at the harbor and lots of laughs— but I can't really shift what I felt. I knew now what it was to be scared. That's a terrible lesson ya have to learn, isn't it? Wastin' life 'cause you're frightened of it. *(Slight pause)* Terrible. *(Slight pause)* I wish I could have the same spirit my ma had. Even half of it be good.

(A pause.)

GIRL: You're a lovely person. *(Slight pause)* I'm very happy my Hoover was broken.
GUY: Me, too.

(There's a tension suddenly. They both know something is about to happen between them. But then:)

GIRL: I like spending time with you . . . but I have certain responsibilities—if sometimes I seem cold . . .
GUY: It's all right—don't worry about it.

(A slight pause.)

GIRL: Ivanka's father is my husband. Is this okay?
GUY: I understand.
GIRL: Tomorrow we will go to the studio and record.
GUY: Yeah.
GIRL: We will do good. Don't be frightened.

(A pause.)

GUY: So what's the Czech for, "Do you still love him?"

(A pause.)

GIRL: Ty ho este miluješ?

GUY: So . . . Ty ho este miluješ?

(A pause. In Czech she answers:)

GIRL: Miluji těbe.

(We read "I love you" in the surtitles.)

GUY: What does that mean?

(She looks up above them.)

GIRL: It looks like rain.

*(She turns away and into a new lighting state.
He begins to play and sing "Sleeping.")*

SLEEPING

GUY:

Are you sleeping?
Still dreaming?
Still drifting off alone.
I'm not leaving with this feeling
So you'd better best be told
And how in the world did you come
To be such a lazy love?

It's so simple and fitting
The path that you are on
We're not talking, there's no secrets
There's just a note that you have gone
And all that you ever owned
Is packed in the hall to go.

And how am I supposed to live without you?
A wrong word said in anger and you were gone.

I'm not listening for signals
It's all dust now on the shelf.

Are you still working? Still counting?
Still buried in yourself?
And how in the world did we come
To have such an absent love?

And how am I supposed to live without you?
A wrong word said in anger and you were gone.
And how am I supposed to live without anyone?

And how in the world did you come
To be such a lazy love?
And where did you go?

(New lighting state.
The studio engineer, Eamon, stands staring at this shabby bunch of misfits.)

EAMON: So has ahhh . . . has any one of yas ever made anythin'
. . . anythin' outside your bedrooms?
GUY: No we're all virgins.
BILLY: Speak for yourself.
BANK MANAGER: Absolutely.
GUY: Studio virgins.
BANK MANAGER: Oh right. Yeah first time.
BILLY: Last night was a night of first times. Last night Eamon . . .
last night I gave my body to the Goddess of Desire. I was
free . . . like a bird—like a giant bird with a beard.
EAMON: Very good.

(Švec is standing very close to Eamon. He looks a little wild-eyed.)

ŠVEC: Hello.
EAMON: Hello. *(Slight pause)* Well ahh . . . well the kitchen's over
there. Help yourselves to tea and coffee.
ŠVEC: Oh yeah coffee yeah!
EAMON: Biscuits you can buy in a little shop around the corner.

ŠVEC: Little shop-deadly-great—I love biscuits!

EAMON: You're all miked-up so . . . em . . . what are we recording?

ŠVEC: Songs, Eamon! Masses of songs . . .

EAMON: Are you on drugs? Is he on drugs?! We don't allow drugs in here?

ŠVEC: That real coffee in your kitchen?

EAMON: Yeah, what about it?

ŠVEC: I drank it.

EAMON: Ya drank it all?

ŠVEC: Most definitely. I can't feel me legs. Andrej!

(Andrej releases some anger and punches Švec hard in the leg.)

Nothing.

BILLY *(To the Bank Manager)*: She lay upon me like a sensuous ninja. So athletic and yet so generous with her body.

BANK MANAGER: I'm not a huge fan of breasts.

BILLY: Fair enough.

BANK MANAGER: More of a penis person.

BILLY: That's tricky to find on a woman. *(A slight pause. The penny drops)* Understood.

ANDREJ *(To Eamon)*: Your sweetest dream will be stolen from you . . . and life . . . will grind . . . your bones . . . to dust.

(Slight pause.)

EAMON *(To the Girl)*: How long's this session?

GIRL: Twenty-four-hour lock-in.

EAMON: Fuck me. Right, well let's get started!

(Eamon leaves the light.
The Guy turns to his band.)

GUY: Okay. *(To the Girl)* So you're with me from the start. Billy, Švec, Andrej you're in on the second verse— *(To the Bank Manager)* I'll give ya a nod.

(The Guy and Girl exchange a look.)

And we know what we're doing, right?

GIRL: Right.

(The Guy and the Girl begin to play "When Your Mind's Made Up.")

WHEN YOUR MIND'S MADE UP

GUY AND GIRL:
> So, if you ever want something
> And you call, call
> Then I'll come running
> To fight and I'll be at your door
> When there's nothing worth running for
>
> When your mind's made up
> When your mind's made up
> There's no point trying to change it
>
> When your mind's made up
> When your mind's made up
> There's no point trying to stop it, you see

(Billy, Švec and Andrej are in and miraculously they play sweetly.)

> You're just like everyone
> When the shit falls
> All you wanna do is run away
> And hide all by yourself
> When there's far from, there's nothing else
>
> When your mind's made up
> When your mind's made up
> There's no point trying to change it
>
> When your mind's made up
> When your mind's made up
> There's no point even talking

When your mind's made up
When your mind's made up
There's no point trying to fight it

When your mind's, your mind
Love, love
There's no point trying to change it
When your love

So if you ever want something
And you call, call
Then I'll come running.

(Eamon walks into the light, stunned. A pause.
Eamon: Wow. That was nice. Did you write that?)

GUY: Yeah.
EAMON: Wow.

(The Guy turns to the Girl. She's smiling at him. It was wonderful.)

Take a breath, we'll go for another one.

(A lighting change.
Suddenly the Girl's alone at the piano. She plays and sings "The
Hill.")

THE HILL

GIRL:

Walking up the hill tonight
When you have closed your eyes
I wish I didn't have to make all those mistakes and be wise
Please try to be patient and know that I'm still learning
I'm sorry that you have to see the strength inside me
    burning

But where are you my angel now
Don't you see me crying
And I know that you can't do it all
But you can't say I'm not trying
I'm on my knees in front of him
But he doesn't seem to see me
With all his troubles on his mind he's looking right
    through me
And I'm letting myself down beside this fire in you
And I wish that you could see I have my troubles, too

(The Guy is coming into the light, unseen by her.)

Lookin' at you sleeping
I'm with a man I know
I'm sitting here weeping while the hours pass so slow
And I know that in the mornin' I have to let you go
And you'll be just a man once I used to know
But for these past few days someone I don't recognize
This isn't all my fault
When will you realize

Lookin' at you leavin'.
I'm lookin' for a sign.

GUY: Hey.
GIRL: Hi—are you doing okay?
GUY: Yeah. It's all good.
GIRL: It sounds great.
GUY: Real nice people too, hey?
GIRL: It will be hard to leave.
GUY: Jesus, you're always trying to get rid of me! You mustn't
    like me!
GIRL: I like you. You know I like you.
GUY: That's all right then.

(He takes her hand.
    There's a moment where it looks like they'll kiss but she lowers
her head.)

GIRL: My husband called. He is coming back to Dublin and we will try to work things out.

(His head drops. A slight pause.)

GUY: That's great news.

GIRL: We'll see.

GUY: You'll be grand. It'll be all great.

GIRL: Are you okay?

GUY *(Quickly)*: Jesus I don't know what you're doing! . . .

GIRL: What do you mean?

GUY: You've given me a new life and you're a part of that life and you're just pushing me away . . .

GIRL: You have someone, too!

GUY: Well maybe I do—I don't know yet—but that's not important! . . .

GIRL: It is unfinished between you.

GUY: And so what?!

GIRL: You cannot walk through your life leaving unfinished love behind you! You have all this heart in these songs and it is because of this girl in New York. It is for you and your love that we make this tape.

GUY: But what about us and this moment! Isn't this unfinished?

GIRL: But we haven't started anything.

(A slight pause.)

GUY: No? Well it feels like we've started.

(A slight pause.)

Fuck I'm saying this to you now 'cause maybe I'll never get a chance—but you've turned love around for me and you've done it in five days. And yeah I wrote these songs at another time for another girl, but when I sing it's for us, I think—it's you I see in the songs . . .

GIRL: I don't want you to talk like that!

GUY: Why not?!

GIRL: Because it can't be about that!

(A pause.)

GUY: Okay fine.

(He quickly leaves.
New lighting state.
The sound of the sea.
The Girl stands on one side of the stage and the Guy on the other.
Billy, the Bank Manager, Švec, Andrej and Eamon stand
between them, looking out to sea.
Unaccompanied, unprompted, Billy begins to sing "Gold.")

GOLD

BILLY:

> And I love her so
> I wouldn't trade her for gold
> I'm walking on moonbeams
> I was born with a silver spoon

(The Bank Manager, Švec, Andrej and Eamon accompany a
cappella.)

BILLY, ŠVEC, ANDREJ, EAMON AND THE BANK MANAGER:

> And I'm gonna be me
> I'm gonna be free
> I'm walking on moonbeams
> And staring out to sea
>
> And if a door be closed
> Then a row of homes start building
> And tear your curtains down
> For sunlight is like gold
>
> And you better be you
> And do what you can do
> When you're walking on moonbeams
> Staring out to sea.

(A slight pause.)

BILLY: She's a lovely woman Réza. Kind. A little out of my league probably.

BANK MANAGER: Well you can only try.

BILLY: Yeah.

(A slight pause.)

But how do people come and stay together, I wonder? It's a complicated business this "love."

BANK MANAGER: That's the problem. Love's all very well, but in the hands of people it turns into soup.

BILLY: That's often true yeah. Still.

BANK MANAGER: Yeah.

(A slight pause.)

BILLY: Are you married, Eamon?

EAMON: Yeah I am actually.

BANK MANAGER: Still in love?

EAMON: Yeah.

BILLY: Fair play to ya, that's great.

EAMON: Is yeah.

BILLY: Good soup.

(Eamon smiles.
A pause.)

ŠVEC: Look at it lying there, waking up. A little flat city and a new day. *(Slight pause)* Dublin's really lovely.

ANDREJ: A million times heartbroken and Dublin keeps on going. You've got to love Dublin for dreaming.

(A pause.)

EAMON: I better get goin', so . . . You made great music today, boys. Really great. All of yas.

BANK MANAGER: Thanks Eamon.

(A slight pause.)

ŠVEC: Can we get a lift into town with you?

EAMON: Sure, where can I drop yas off?

ŠVEC: A little shot of coffee needed—kick-start the head, hey, bro?

ANDREJ: Lovely.

EAMON: A coffee shop then?

ŠVEC: Bingo.

EAMON: And you guys are all right?

BILLY: Yeah I think I'll walk actually. Stretch the old legs, Eamon.

BANK MANAGER: Me, too.

(Eamon walks away with Švec and Andrej.)

BILLY: Open the shop. Though why bother openin' it up, I don't know.

(A slight pause. The Bank Manager looks at him.)

BANK MANAGER: I can give you some advice. Help you get those bastard bankers off your back.

BILLY: Yeah?

BANK MANAGER: Ya can't have a city without music, Billy. Dublin needs you.

(It's all he's wanted to hear.)

BILLY: Thank you.

BANK MANAGER: Let's walk.

*(Billy walks away with the Bank Manager.
The Guy and Girl look across at each other.
The sound of the waves cross-fades with the sound of the city.
He's holding a bunch of CDs in his hands.)*

GIRL: Can I get one of those CDs? I knew that we would make something good. Are you happy with it?

GUY: Do you want to rob my da's motorbike go for a drive . . .

GIRL: I need to go to Ivanka—I have to give my mother a break . . .
GUY: Yeah of course.

(A pause.)

GIRL: So you'll telephone your girl tonight?
GUY: Yeah.

(A pause.)

Look do you want to come over to mine later, listen to the
CD, talk a bit?
GIRL: A little hanky-panky?
GUY: No one calls it hanky-panky anymore.
GIRL: Maybe that's why I can't find any.
GUY: Yeah you've got to use a different word.
GIRL: That is my problem!
GUY *(Laughing)*: Jesus don't say that!
GIRL *(Laughing)*: Sorry!

(They laugh, both blushing.)

GUY: Come to New York with me! Come on, we'll write loads of
songs together—live in a big flat me, you, Ivanka, and it will
be brilliant!
GIRL: Yeah we go to New York and we will tell no one! And no
one will ever be able to find us again.
GUY: No one! And we'll have a great band and we'll sell out loads
of places and it will be just great.
GIRL: And we'll make an album together.
GUY: Ah, man, I'd love that!
GIRL: And I'll play the piano and do the backing vocals!
GUY: And it'll be brilliant because it will be me and you!
GIRL: It will be me and you and all of this beautiful music!
GUY: Yeah! Come on! Come on, I'm serious!

(A slight pause.)

GIRL: Can I bring my mother?

(He smiles. Life seems all too complicated, the dream immediately evaporates.
A pause.)

GUY: Will you call by later?

(A pause. She smiles.)

GIRL: I'll be there.

(They walk away from each other. They look back and turn away once more.)

THE MOON

GUY AND GIRL:
> Shut the door to the moon and let the birds gather
> Play no more with the fool and let the souls wander

(The light moves onto the Guy and Da in the shop. Da's sitting listening to the CD of the Guy singing.
The song ends, the play button pops up.
A pause.)

GUY: So what do you think? You think it's any good—it's only a demo remember . . .
DA: It's fucking great.
GUY: Yeah?
DA: That'll be a hit, no question—even I can see that—it's magic, Son—brilliant.
GUY: Thanks, Da.

(A pause.)

DA: I saw that ticket—says you're flying tomorrow.
GUY: Listen I'll be straight back if you need me for anything . . .
DA: Don't be daft, I'll be grand . . .
GUY: Honest, Da . . .

DA: Go, Son, do it . . .

GUY: But you'll be all right here alone? . . .

DA: I've got a lot more life in me than I give myself credit for.

GUY: I know you do.

DA: Making moves on Baruška in the studio, d'you see that?

GUY: I saw that.

DA: She's taking me dancing on Friday.

GUY: Seriously?

DA: She's always serious—she's Czech.

GUY: Fair play to ya.

DA: Now here ya go.

(Da hands him a check. The Guy looks at it.)

GUY: Jesus, Da, that's loads! . . .

DA: It's just money—you might need it over there—it'll make you feel brave. Take it, Son.

GUY: Thanks.

(A slight pause.)

DA: So how's the heart?

GUY: It's travelin', Da.

(A pause.)

DA: It will all be great. Everything. Just live. *(Slight pause)* Make your ma proud. *(About the CD)* Now play it again!

(A phone is heard ringing—the Guy alone.
A light fades up on his ex as the phone is answered.)

EX-GIRLFRIEND: Hey there.

GUY: Hi. So how's it goin' over there . . .

EX-GIRLFRIEND: I'm really missing you.

GUY: Yeah?

(A slight pause.)

EX-GIRLFRIEND: So much.

GUY: I'm missing you, too.

(A slight pause.)

Listen I'm coming over there.

EX-GIRLFRIEND: Really?!

GUY: If you want—if you think—

EX-GIRLFRIEND: Just come!

GUY: It's all right then?

EX-GIRLFRIEND: You're joking me!! It's wonderful!

GUY: All right then.

(A slight pause.)

EX-GIRLFRIEND: When will I see you?

GUY: When you wake up tomorrow.

(He looks back in the Girl's direction.
They stare across at each other.)

GIRL *(Softly)*: Go.

("Falling Slowly" is heard over "The Moon" as the light slowly
fades on the Girl.
The Guy knows in that moment that she isn't coming to him.
Their lives must continue.
A new lighting state as the Guy is seen talking to Billy. He
hands him the check his da had given him.
Billy hugs and kisses him.
The light comes back up in the Girl's flat. Andrej is standing
behind her, covering her eyes. Baruška, Réza and Švec are all there.
Billy is wheeling a piano wrapped in a big red bow into the
living room. The piano she loved.
The Guy sings:)

GUY:

> I don't know you
> But I want you
> All the more for that

(Andrej drops his hands. She sees the piano and bursts into surprise.)

> Words fall through me
> And always fool me
> And I can't react
> And games that never amount
> To more than they're meant
> Will play themselves out

(He continues singing.
He could be in the room with her, but he is already gone. She
sits at the piano and plays and sings with him:)

GUY AND GIRL:

> Take this sinking boat and point it home
> We've still got time
> Raise your hopeful voice you have a choice
> You've made it now
> Falling slowly, eyes that know me
> And I can't go back
> Moods that take me and erase me
> And I'm painted black
> You have suffered enough
> And warred with yourself
> It's time that you won
> Take this sinking boat and point it home
> We've still got time
> Raise your hopeful voice you have the choice
> You've made it now
> Falling slowly sing your melody
> I'll sing it loud.

Take it all.
I played the cards too late,
Now it's gone.

(They are lost in the song and its music.
The delicate strains of "Falling Slowly" fade away as the light
fades.
Blackout.)

END

ENDA WALSH (Book) is an Irish playwright living in London. He is the winner of numerous international awards, and his work has been translated and produced worldwide. His plays include *Misterman, Penelope, The New Electrical Ballroom, The Walworth Farce, Chatroom, The Small Things, bedbound, Disco Pigs, How These Desperate Men Talk, Lynndie's Gotta Gun, Gentrification, My Friend Duplicity* and *Room 303*. He co-wrote the screenplay for *Hunger* (directed and co-written by Steve McQueen, 2008). Walsh was awarded the Tony Award and the Outer Critic Circle Award for his work on *Once*.

GLEN HANSARD (Music and Lyrics) is a musician/songwriter and actor, who wrote songs for the musical and film versions of *Once*, for which he won an Academy Award for Best Original Song for "Falling Slowly." He also starred in the film and had a role in *The Commitments*. His albums include *The Swell Season, Strict Joy, The Cost, Burn the Maps, Set List: Live in Dublin, For the Birds, Dance the Devil, Fitzcarraldo* and *Another Love Song*. He also wrote songs for *The Hunger Games*. He is a member of The Swell Season and The Frames. He recently released his first solo album, *Rhythm and Repose*.

MARKÉTA IRGLOVÁ (Music and Lyrics) is a musician/songwriter and actress, who wrote songs for the musical and film versions of *Once*, for which she won an Academy Award for Best Original Song for "Falling Slowly." She also starred in the film *Once*. Her albums include *The Swell Season, Strict Joy* and her solo debut *Anar*.